How Now

How Now

100 ways to celebrate
the present moment

RAPHAEL CUSHNIR

...

Photographs *by* Pornchai Mittongtare

CHRONICLE BOOKS
SAN FRANCISCO

Library of Congress Cataloging-in-Publication Data available.

ISBN 0-8118-4861-2

Manufactured in China

Design by Jay Peter Salvas
This book was typeset in the text face Mrs. Eaves 10/13½ and
Shelly Andante 13½.

Distributed in Canada by Raincoast Books
9050 Shaughnessy Street
Vancouver, British Columbia V6P 6E5

10 9 8 7 6 5 4 3 2 1

Chronicle Books LLC
85 Second Street
San Francisco, California 94105

www.chroniclebooks.com
www.hownow100.com

This book is dedicated to all the counseling clients and workshop participants I've had the honor to serve. Your courage and presence provide me with boundless inspiration. With each of these hundred celebrations, I celebrate you as well.

Table of Contents

INTRODUCTION

You already know how important it is to live in the present moment. Philosophers, sages, poets, and mystics have been making the point for centuries. "Seize the day," wrote Horace. "You can never step in the same river twice," proclaimed Heracleitus. "Be here now," exhorted Ram Dass, inspiring the entire '60s generation in the process.

But what does living in the moment really look like? Feel like? And, most important, how does one actually do it?

The good news is that it's simple. The bad news is that it's not always easy. But there's more good news—the ability to stay in the Now can be easily learned and strengthened over time like a muscle. Even the briefest moments of presence can quickly lead to more presence. Eventually, living in the moment becomes a natural, effortless way of life.

As the saying goes, "There's no time like the present." So let's begin. Take a breath. Pay attention to the way the air feels as it fills your lungs and expands your belly. Now relax, and let the next breath come on its own. Do you feel just a bit more here? The simple act of breathing attentively can always lead you back to the Now.

Look around the location in which you're reading. Keep looking without any goal in mind until your eyes land upon something you haven't noticed before. Once you've found it, go see if it has a smell. If it does, let the smell linger in your nose. If it doesn't, follow your nose to the closest thing that has a smell.

Tapping into your senses is another quick way to become more fully present. Smell, sight, hearing, touch, and taste all work well. In addition to the external five senses, there is also your ability to sense within, to experience the way your body internally registers pleasure, pain, hunger, fullness, and other sensations. For example, pay attention to what happens when you smile. Notice how your interior sensations shift as a result. Next, close your mouth and hum a note. Follow the vibration of the sound waves as they spread through your organs and bones. Let them wake you up.

While awareness of your breath and senses is instrumental in true presence, there's much more to it than that. Unfortunately, we spend a large part of our lives blocking out what we don't want to acknowledge and accept. Feelings, difficult situations, troubling aspects of the world at large—all these can cause us to shut down, to turn away from what's actually happening. Whenever this occurs, we lose our connection to the present moment. In the process, we also lose our vitality, our innate joy, and our power to heal and grow.

Most of the time, our disconnection from the present moment is unconscious. We're gone and don't know it, or we know we're gone but don't know why. That's where this book comes in. These hundred ways to celebrate the present moment are designed to help you find out when, where, and why you might have shut down, and then to bring you back to life as swiftly and enjoyably as possible.

The best way to approach presence is with a playful spirit. It's about freedom, after all. So rather than putting *How Now* on your to-do list, just pick it up from time to time and turn to a random page. Read the page slowly, like a poem, letting the words and practices sink in.

No matter in what order you approach the hundred ways, and no matter how long you take to complete them, their effect will be cumulative. Each of the ways will reinforce the others. At a level deeper than everyday awareness, your being will begin to blossom. You will feel more peace, love, and contentment than you previously thought possible.

This is the gift that the present moment bestows. Always. And it's yours right now.

BEGIN

In the trance of habit and daily routine, it's easy to miss the miracle of existence that is continually unfolding. One way to reconnect to that miracle is to consciously bring new projects and activities into your life. Whether tiny or grand, every venture you begin provides a fresh invitation to savor the Now.

The Practice:

Make a list of some endeavors that you'd like to begin. This list can include an array of choices, such as a new friendship, an herb garden, a dance class, a journal, a different style of dress, a book you've always wanted to read, or a more honest way of communicating. Your selections can also be internally oriented, such as paying more attention to what you feel or focusing on what brings you joy.

Next, scan the list for something you can begin right now. Do so, and allow yourself to bask in its birth. Then keep the list nearby and make frequent beginnings an ongoing part of your life. Refresh the list often as you grow and change.

Although the process of thinking can seem straightforward, it's anything but. Thoughts come in an infinite variety. Some thoughts arise as words, others as whole concepts, and still others as images. Many thoughts are a blend of these three types, differing in length, proportion, and intensity. Any full-fledged stream of thought will likely include an array of such combinations. Watching your thoughts as if they were a three-dimensional inner movie can bring you much closer than usual to your moment-by-moment state of consciousness.

The Practice:

Relax. Close your eyes. Watch your thoughts for the next two minutes. Pay less attention to their content than to their form. Notice in particular whether they appear as words, concepts, images, or combinations. Now open your eyes and repeat. Does the form of your thoughts change when accompanied by external sight?

CULTIVATE GRATITUDE

Gratitude opens our minds and hearts. It instantly connects us to the present moment. Plus, it feels absolutely wonderful. The fact that gratitude is so easy to come by gives us one more reason to be grateful.

The Practice:

Make a list of ten things for which you're grateful. Once the list is complete, let yourself actually *feel* gratitude for each item. Keep this list by your bedside and look it over each morning and evening. Every time you recognize another thing for which you're grateful, add it to the list. Watch how gratitude increases in direct proportion to your focus on it.

INNER SMILE

Feeling joyful is not necessary for presence, but it's one of the most powerful ways to induce it. Joy creates an almost instantaneous sense of expansion—an inner smile that's like a warm bath. Some call this warm bath "flow" or "spirit." Experiencing it connects us to ourselves and to everyone and everything around us.

The Practice:

Think about someone or something that you love. This could be a child, a place in nature, or a favorite memory. Whatever you choose, make sure that just reflecting upon it creates an automatic inner smile. Then surrender to that inner smile. Let it light you up. Feel it spread through your body and even beyond it, uniting you joyously with your surroundings.

BREATHING BY NUMBERS

Your breath is a direct connection to the Now, and to life itself. Although you ordinarily think of yourself as an independent individual, every inhale and exhale is a literal bridge between what's within you and what's outside you. The more aware you grow of your breathing, the more robust that bridge becomes.

The Practice:

Breathe naturally, at your own pace, and count your breaths up to ten. Sounds simple, right? Yet most likely you'll lose track many times along the way. This happens to almost everyone. It's a function of our wandering minds. When it does happen, begin again without frustration or worry. Counting your breaths is not a game to win or a skill to master, but rather an opportunity to grow. Growth happens in its own way and at its own rhythm.

Perform this practice when you wake up, on your way to work, and at any other time you're not otherwise occupied. Once you're able to keep track of ten breaths, try increasing your count to twenty.

SHOWER WITH PRAISE

Like a rollicking belly laugh, presence is contagious. Often, when you help someone else feel fully alive, it wakes up your own spirit as well.

The Practice:

Choose someone in your life who's been struggling lately, who may have lost touch with the kind of confidence and ease that can come only from within. Next, think about what you most admire or appreciate about the person. Perhaps it's kindness, enthusiasm, or the tendency to crack a joke when people take themselves too seriously.

Now is the time for you to share. Offer your praise in person if possible, but if not, just pick up the phone. Make it clear that you have no agenda in communicating other than to express your appreciation. Notice how it feels to speak the words. Notice whether they create joy, embarrassment, a combination of the two, or something else entirely. Then, over the next few weeks, notice whether the entire relationship changes at all. Finally, notice whether any of your other relationships are affected as well.

DANCE LIKE MAD

No moment stands still, and neither should we. There is functional movement, there is mindless movement, and then there is dance. Dancing connects us with flow, with spirit, and, almost instantly, with the Now. In order to reap the gifts dance has to offer, we don't need to be skillful at it—just willing.

The Practice:

Wear clothes that don't restrict your movement. Make sure you're in a room without mirrors. Put on music that fits your mood. Warm up your body with a few minutes of stretching. Now you're ready to let loose.

Dancing comes naturally to most of us, so little instruction is required. Many people, however, have a hard time leaving behind feelings of awkwardness and self-consciousness. Therefore, let this dance come from the inside out. That means your intent is not to look good but to express whatever arises in each moment. If you feel clumsy, for instance, let that clumsiness be a part of the dance. While getting the hang of this, try exaggerating all your movements. Sing along to the melody. Eventually, lose yourself in the dance so that it happens without any forethought.

OUT WITH THE OLD

The past clutters up our homes as well as our minds. Often we feel hemmed in, trapped by all our accumulated stuff. Letting go of some of that stuff on a regular basis creates room to breathe, stretch out, and welcome what's fresh and new.

The Practice:

Give yourself a day to open every drawer, cupboard, and closet in your home. Inventory all your stuff with an eye toward letting it go. If you absolutely need something, leave it where it is. If you haven't used something in a year and have no emotional attachment to it, put it in a "recycle" pile. If you haven't used it in a year but do have an emotional attachment to it, put it in a "maybe" pile.

Spend a little time with each item in the maybe pile. Let the feelings connected to it flow. Notice whether the attachment is one that seems to shut you down or open you up. If it's the former, consider adding that item to the recycle pile.

Then, when you're all done, recycle everything you're ready to let go of, and revel in your newfound spaciousness.

DIG IN THE DIRT

Every living creature owes its very existence to the planet we inhabit. Humans, however, are the only species that has learned to survive without a direct connection to the earth. We accomplished this by creating a system in which a small sector of the population provides our food and other earthly resources. While there's great efficiency in this system, it often disconnects us from our primal, animal nature. On the other hand, all it takes is a little mud under the fingernails to restore that missing link.

The Practice:

On a warm, sunny day, find a patch of dirt that's soft and moist. Bring along a shovel, rake, or hoe to get things started. Loosen the dirt with your tool and then set the tool aside. Sit or lie down right on the ground so you can feel the earth against your body. Then start digging with ungloved hands. Let there be no purpose to this digging except exploration. Explore what the soil smells like and how it crumbles on your fingers. Be as gentle and undisruptive as possible to any fellow creatures, such as worms or beetles you encounter. Don't stop your dig until you *feel* like the animal that you truly are.

SLOW DOWN

The speed of contemporary life is fierce. Human beings weren't made for it. Even those of us who thrive on multitasking and channel surfing place an enormous strain on our bodies, which haven't evolved for such activity. Taking specific time out to move through life at a pace that matches our physical and evolutionary wiring provides two benefits. First, it's a recalibration that leads to luscious and immediate presence. And second, it recharges us to handle all those other moments when slowing down isn't really an option.

The Practice:

Choose an activity that you're able to perform at least three times slower than usual. Cooking, walking, and bathing are three such possibilities. Give yourself more than enough time for this practice so that nothing will impinge on it.

Make sure to breathe, pause, ponder, and move through your activity with gentle and continuous attention. If the urge to speed up arises, stop completely until it passes. Once you're in a relaxed and easy flow, let yourself surrender to the flow rather than dictate it.

PRECIOUS PEOPLE

No one ever went to the grave wishing to have loved less. In the end, it's the people in our lives who matter most. Yet often, out of fear or pain, we don't let them know that. Taking time to do so allows what's truest in our hearts to be acknowledged and celebrated in the Now.

The Practice:

Who are the most important people in your life? Reflect on this question in a relaxed manner, even if the answers are surprising or seem somehow inappropriate. Rather than focusing on whom you "should" love, let your heart have the last word.

Then, over the next few weeks, make it a point to communicate to those people exactly how you feel. Do it in a way that's natural for you, and that they can most easily hear and accept. Is the vulnerability that comes with such revelation easy for you, or does it take a little getting used to?

SKIP LIKE A FIVE-YEAR-OLD

Your body knows how to play even when you don't. Just a smidgen of willingness is all it needs to let loose. Often, a few moments of uninhibited play jog loose what was stuck, bringing creativity, ease, and joy where they previously seemed impossible.

The Practice:

Skip—that's all there is to it. Whether in public or private, make sure you've got ample room in which to get up a good head of steam. Skip your way through the embarrassment, the self-consciousness, and all your self-judgments about silliness and wasting time. Skip until you're out of breath. Skip until you can't help but feel a bounding sense of glee.

COLOR SCAN

If you find yourself out of sorts, lost in turmoil and therefore far removed from the present moment, a quick and effective remedy is always available. Engaging in a rapid-fire activity that requires both sensory awareness and intense concentration can jolt you out of even the most daunting distress.

The Practice:

For thirty seconds, take in all the sights around you. As quickly as possible during that time, name every object you see along with its color—such as "Blue wall, brown chair, yellow grapefruit, red placemat. When you're finished, take a deep breath and notice whether you're more centered and present. If not, move to a different room and repeat the practice.

FIND A FIRST

In Zen, **beginner's mind** *refers to a quality of openness, a consistent willingness to see things in a new way and to change course accordingly. Beginner's mind stems from the realization that every single moment carries something distinctive within it. As you become accustomed to this perspective, it's helpful not just to see new things, but to bring new things into your experience as well.*

The Practice:

On each of the next few days, do something you've never done before. Rather than selecting a longterm project, as suggested in *Begin* (PAGE 13), choose something—whether modest or grand—that you can complete right then and there. The possibilities are endless. You might smile at your perpetually grumpy coworker, eat a new food, or prepare a familiar one differently. Perhaps you'll try that strange piece of equipment at the gym, give someone a gift for absolutely no reason, or parachute out of a plane. As you accomplish each new first, see if it renders you a bit more lively and alert.

TASTE TEST

The more attention you pay to your body, the more present you automatically become. Physical presence is the gateway to a whole new level of wellness. This is clearest, perhaps, when it comes to food. Most of us select what we eat via a combination of desires and "shoulds." Rarely do we tap into our bodies' instant feedback mechanism to identify the right food at the right moment.

The Practice:

For just one day, put your first bite of any food under your tongue and hold it there for twenty seconds before swallowing. Notice any and all sensations that occur in your body. If you feel even just a tad worse than you did before, your body is saying, "No, thank you."

When this does happen, see if you can override any competing desires and lay the food aside. If you can't, don't stress about it. Rather, watch for any repercussions over the next few days, such as headaches or irritability. If you spot any, this may make it easier to choose differently next time.

CLOUD FIGURES

Leisure time *used to mean those parts of the week when few activities were planned. Nowadays it's morphed into a few hours into which we schedule our hobbies, entertainment, and "play dates." In the process, we lose the vital opportunity to reflect and rejuvenate. Fortunately, we can get it back in the blink of an eye.*

The Practice:

Wait for a cloudy day. Find a comfortable spot outside where you can lie on your back and look up aimlessly at the sky. Let the clouds drift across your field of vision. Notice the speed at which the wind carries them and the way they shift and merge into one another. Without trying to see anything in particular, notice if your mind overlays the clouds with faces or figures. Whatever happens, enjoy the languid experience. Treasure these rare moments when all you have to do is be.

GET LOST

Having a sense of control over our lives is a powerful human need. For most of us, however, this need becomes exaggerated. We try to control far more than is ever possible, and this attempt is like a vice grip that can squeeze presence right out of our existence. Creating situations in which we're purposely out of control *is a great way to tip the scales back toward the Now.*

The Practice:

Head to a part of town that you don't know well. Check in advance that the area is safe. Park your car, if you're driving, and note the nearest intersection. Then walk and walk and walk until you're good and lost. Keep walking, without making any attempt to get your bearings. Don't consult a map. Take in all your surroundings with curious eyes and an open mind.

Notice especially any feelings of discomfort or apprehension that arise from being so far off your beaten path. If such feelings do arise, just let them be and keep breathing. After an hour or two, find a local resident and ask for directions back to your starting point. On the way home, consider whether the experience woke up, or shook up, any dormant aspects of yourself.

PLAY WITH YOUR VOICE

The human voice is like an orchestra, capable of an infinite variety of sounds. Each sound the voice makes connects us to a different emotional or sensory state. Taking our voices beyond their usual range brings a sense of deeper possibility to each passing moment.

The Practice:

Find a location where no one else can hear you. Then start humming, whooping, chirping, and clucking, making every sound that comes to mind. Range all across the scale, from deep bass to high falsetto, from faint whisper to full volume. Let one sound shift into another until you don't know what's coming next, until the sounds are leading *you*.

SINGULAR FOCUS

Almost all spiritual traditions recommend some kind of concentration practice to increase our depth of presence . The object upon which we concentrate isn't really important. What matters is that we remain gently and consistently focused.

The Practice:

Select an object of concentration such as a candle flame or a spot on the wall. Look at this object for ten minutes. Focus your whole being on the object, returning to this focus whenever your thoughts drift. Melt gradually into this practice until the object and observer begin to merge.

SHARE A HARD TRUTH

Telling the truth when we feel vulnerable is one of the hardest things to do. We might fear rejection, abandonment, disapproval, disappointment, rage, hurt, or just the raw exposure that's an unavoidable part of the process. Yet almost every time we're willing to tell a hard truth, we grow and deepen in presence, no matter the response. The energy that we previously locked up to maintain a false front is now freed to uplift and enliven us.

The Practice:

Think about the various people in your life—family, friends, coworkers, and community members. In what relationship have you been bottling up a hard truth? This truth may be about something you're feeling or not feeling, or about a part of the relationship that isn't working for you.

Look at the list of fears in the first paragraph above. Are you holding back due to one or more of those fears? Are you willing to experience that fear and still tell your hard truth? If so, pick a time and place where both you and the other person have the best chance of hearing each other without blame or recrimination. Once it's all over and the dust has settled, notice whether you feel lighter.

WIDEN YOUR AWARENESS

Most of the time, our attention is focused outward on what we're doing or encountering in the world. Sometimes we turn our attention inward to note what we feel physically. In the flow of life, we alternate unconsciously between these two aspects of presence. Yet it's possible to widen our awareness and focus on both realms simultaneously. By mastering this skill, we become more consistently in touch with the information and wisdom our bodies provide.

The Practice:

Seek out a friendly conversation. While you're listening to your conversation partner, widen your awareness to include your own ongoing physical sensations. You might, for example, feel peaceful, anxious, sad, warm, or tense. Your response to what you hear might bring about frequent shifts of sensation. The goal is to experience an easy back-and-forth flow between all those sensations and your partner's words.

In addition, widen your awareness when you're the one speaking in the conversation. What percentage of the time are you able to stay connected to what's happening within yourself? Is that connection easier when you listen or when you speak? Either way, the more you experiment with this practice, the easier it will become.

VOLUNTARY SHUTDOWN

Whenever we don't like or want something, we instinctively recoil from it. This is true of both the tiniest annoyances and the hugest traumas. There's nothing wrong with this process — it's natural and unavoidable. But remaining shut down past the initial recoil creates a lasting barrier to presence. Learning to become aware of our shut-downs is the first step in decreasing their impact.

The Practice:

Think of something that really frustrates you. Choose an issue that you've already struggled mightily to resolve. Let all the frustration associated with this issue fill you up completely, then turn your attention to your body and notice exactly what you feel and where you feel it. This might be a tension in your shoulders, a gnawing in your gut, or a clenching of your jaw.

This feeling is a shutdown. The way you feel it is probably the way you most often feel when you shut down. Knowing this, you can now turn the sensation into a call for presence. Whenever it arises, use the technique in *Befriend Your Pain (Revisited)* (PAGE 96) to get to the heart of the matter.

Note: If you want to immediately reverse the frustration caused by this exercise and save the deeper work for later, go directly to *Inner Smile* (PAGE 15).

NEIGHBORHOOD WATCH

Life is infinitely fascinating and diverse. The more you look, the more there is to discover. But most of the time, rushing through our daily schedules, we block out a majority of what's happening all about us. Setting aside a few moments to look around, with no particular agenda, can add renewed luster to our everyday experience.

The Practice:

Find a place near your home that's ideal for hanging out—perhaps a park bench, a bus stop, or the parking lot of a supermarket. Camp there for at least twenty minutes. Watch everything that happens, paying particular attention to what you ordinarily might not see when you're on the go.

If it feels uncomfortable to be so idle, let the sensations of discomfort remain, and keep watching. If you get bored, let your boredom be part of the experience, too. As you watch, take note of any unusual or unexpected sights, sounds, sensations, or reflections. See if they cause you to experience anything previously familiar in a new or different way.

COMMUNICATE WITH PURE SOUND

Human beings constantly load meanings and interpretations on top of the raw experience of the Now. From time to time, limiting our use of words with those we love can help break through what's become stale, contentious, or stuck.

The Practice:

Choose a friend you trust and who has a playful sense of humor. Find a convenient hour in which you both agree to communicate with each other using only one-syllable sounds. These sounds could include "Mmmmm," "Ow!" "Grrrrr," and "Ahhhh." Avoid one-syllable words that have a specific meaning different from what the actual sounds convey, including, for example, "Yes" and "No."

DRAW WITH YOUR OPPOSITE HAND

Inside every one of us there's a wild-eyed, innocent child for whom each day offers new chances to learn, grow, try, fail, and try again. We can always evoke this child by purposely performing a task at which we're blessedly bumbling beginners.

The Practice:

Using a big sheet of paper and a marker, write your name a number of times with your nondominant hand. Let the resulting awkwardness take you over. Have fun with it. Then, draw with the same hand for at least ten minutes. Fully embrace whatever thoughts, emotions, memories, and associations arise.

BE MOVED

Becoming fully present involves connection with universal rhythms that lie outside the boundaries of ordinary awareness. In order to make this connection, we need to quiet our own rhythms and step away from the part of ourselves that commonly dictates our choices and actions. The result of such surrender is almost always inspirational.

The Practice:

Begin by turning on some music and standing completely still. Listen to the music intently but without strain for about five minutes. Allow it to move through your body like air through a screen door. In this state of extreme openness, see if your body is *danced* at all by the music. You might find yourself swaying a little from side to side, rocking out, or remaining stock-still the whole time. The point is to learn what happens when you're not choosing, when you make yourself fully available, body and soul, to the moment at hand.

Repeat this practice three times, with very different types of music.

MODES OF INTUITION

Intuition is the sixth sense. The more we tap into it, the more alive to each moment we become. Everyone has intuition, but we each experience it differently. Recognizing your own personal way of intuiting allows you to call upon this vital human trait with clarity and consistency.

The Practice:

Think back on the last time you felt totally certain about something but couldn't tell how this certainty was reached. What was the corresponding sensation that arrived along with that certainty? Was it a gut feeling? A tingling? A tug at the heart? An inner voice? An undeniable knowing? All or some combination of the above? These are the main signs of intuition. They might vary depending on the situation, but there's usually a common thread.

Over the next few days, keep an eye out for any of these sensations and see if you can discern the basic form of your own intuition. If nothing shows up, wait patiently for the next time you feel strongly about something for no partic- ular reason. Notice the experience that accompanies your strong feeling. Chances are that this experience is one of the main modes of your intuition.

PENETRATE IMPATIENCE

What, exactly, is impatience? It's our rejection of the current moment as it is because something that we want to happen in a future moment hasn't yet occurred. We experience this constantly, in traffic jams and long lines, during commercials, or when a longwinded friend just won't get to the point. Rarely, however, does impatience make the desired experience arrive any faster. What it does instead is deprive us of the pleasures of presence. Luckily, just a slight shift of awareness can reverse this self-imposed loss.

The Practice:

The next time you find yourself impatient, turn your attention to your body and note where that sensation is actually located. It might be in the chest, for example, or the stomach, or the neck and shoulders. Once you've found it, keep your attention placed gently on the sensation until it begins to ease. And that's the amazing part—it almost always does.

Once you no longer feel so gripped by your impatience, use your liberated awareness to reconnect with what's around you—sights, smells, weather, people. Is there anything at all in this current moment that makes waiting just a little more tolerable?

REASONS FOR BEING

Beyond obvious goals, such as making a living or taking care of our loved ones, each of us has one or more essential reasons for being. Here are some common reasons: to love, to learn, to serve others, to heal, to create, to enjoy life. Knowing your reasons for being makes the act of being a more graceful and joyous experience.

The Practice:

Find a quiet moment. Ask yourself, *What are my reasons for being?* When an idea comes up, say it out loud and see if it rings true. Notice what happens in your heart, your gut, and throughout your body in the wake of this statement. It might take a few tries before you strike gold. You know you've found a true reason for being when your body says, "Yes!" Your own personal *yes* might come as a knowing, a sense of peace, or a surge of uplifting energy.

For the next week, repeat your reason for being each morning before you get out of bed. Imagine it permeating every cell in your body. Then, throughout the day, notice whether you live more "on purpose."

MIND YOUR MONEY

What is money? For some it's a blessing, for some it's a curse, and for others it's simply a means of exchange. In one sense, the way you spend money is the irrefutable record of what you value. Watching your expenses over time provides an opportunity to become more present to previously habitual choices. This awareness might be confirming, surprising, or a powerful inducement to change.

The Practice:

For one month, keep a rubber band around the bills in your wallet. Place additional rubber bands around your checkbook, credit card, and ATM card. Then, whenever you have to remove one of the rubber bands in order to buy something, use that moment to reflect. *Do I really care about what I'm buying? What is its impact on my life as a whole? Would I be better served by using this money in another way?*

It's important to note that there's no right or wrong in this exercise. How you spend your money is entirely up to you. So keep your exploration relaxed and light. Let it guide you to your heart's desire.

ENERGY BALL

Within every moment are unseen forces that play a role in what unfolds. Some of them will forever remain a mystery. Others, while seemingly mysterious, are more tangible than we realize. One of these is the force commonly referred to as subtle energy. It's what powers acupuncture, Reiki, and many other types of healing practices. Becoming aware of subtle energy, and our own innate ability to sense it, helps us to recognize how much more is always present than what meets the eye.

The Practice:

Place your palms about a half-inch apart. Tune into the field of subtle energy that naturally exists between them. Sensing it might happen right away or take a few moments. Once you can feel it, gradually move your palms about six inches apart, focusing on the subtle energy that remains in the space created. Now curve your fingers and shape the energy into a ball. Begin to experiment with this energy ball, pressing it, stretching it, and seeing how far you can expand it before the sensation dissipates.

EYE CONTACT

Although the spoken word is our most common way of connecting, it's also possible to get lost in words or to hide behind them. Eye contact, by contrast, is immediate. It can cut through all our defenses and bring us heart to heart. And it can quickly reveal any personal or interpersonal issues that might be in the way.

The Practice:

For one whole day, make direct eye contact with every individual who crosses your path. Allow the gaze to last at least a full second. Include people you know as well as those you don't. If someone won't meet your gaze, just smile and move on. With each gaze, simply acknowledge and appreciate the humanity shared by you and the other person. Notice what happens in each encounter. How does it make you feel? How does it change what transpires?

FIVE-SECOND DELAY

Many things we say and do are split-second reactions to something we've just experienced. By reacting in such a quick and automatic fashion, we lose the opportunity to take in these experiences more fully. The discipline of waiting and witnessing often yields treasures. It can free us from entrenched patterns and reveal whole new ways of being.

The Practice:

For one day, before saying or doing anything, pause for five seconds. While waiting, pay very close attention to the thoughts that cross your mind and to the physical and emotional sensations in your body. Note everything you come across, without analysis or judgment. See if the five-second delay changes anything for you. If there are moments when you can't make it to five seconds, and it's not because someone needs your immediate response, identify which part of the experience became intolerable. Let the answer be a signpost for further exploration. Begin that exploration when the time is right with *Befriend Your Pain (Revisited)* (PAGE 96).

THE HEART MEDITATION

An abundance of love is available in every moment, but we have to be present to receive it. No matter what's blocking us—stress, fear, abandonment, loss—reconnecting to the experience of love is always possible. Contrary to common belief, it doesn't require the participation of another. In fact, it's best achieved alone.

The Practice:

Choose a quiet place where you won't be interrupted. Begin by noticing your breathing. Don't attempt to regulate it in any way. Just get comfortable with its natural rhythm.

Now, on each inhale, imagine that you're taking all the love of the universe directly into your own heart. You might envision that love as a golden light, a cascading waterfall— whatever resonates most for you. In the small pause before exhaling, allow yourself to bask in love's extraordinary glow.

On each exhale, imagine yourself sending all that love directly from your own heart right back to its source. Continue in this way for about five minutes. Breathe in—love. Breathe out— love. If you practice the heart meditation for just a few weeks, you'll find that falling in love with your deepest self and falling in love with all of existence are actually the very same thing.

HONORING CYCLES

Time usually feels linear, but it isn't. It bends, twists, and cycles like the seasons. When Ecclesiastes wrote, "There is nothing new under the sun," he was referring to the way things come back around again and again and again. But every time they do, it's we who are different. That's why honoring cycles is a great way to accentuate the Now.

The Practice:

Pause to assess your life's cycles. They begin, moment by moment, with the inhale and exhale of your breath and the steady beat of your heart. They continue with the flow of your days and the days of your week. They include monthly, seasonal, and yearly occasions, as well as recurring events unique to your own experience.

Choose an upcoming life-cycle occasion that ordinarily passes without much notice. This could be anything from the springtime bloom of your favorite flower to the anniversary of a loved one's passing. When the event next arrives, take a few minutes to consider how you've changed since the last time it came. Consider as well if there's a particular change you'd like to make by the time it comes back once more.

ONE-MINUTE BODY MERGE

Whenever we're in a state of high stress or extreme emotional reaction, our thoughts become rapid and obsessional. They spin us out of the present moment and into a panicky netherworld. Most of the time, however, finding our way back to the Now requires only a simple reconnection with our bodies.

The Practice:

If you find yourself in such a state of extreme anxiety, stop what you're doing and place your attention on your toes. Once you're able to feel sensation within them, move on to your arches, heels, and ankles. When you can feel all of those, continue upward to your calves, knees, thighs, groin, buttocks, and hips. Keep going, and keep breathing, as you feel the presence of your stomach, lower back, chest, upper back, shoulders, neck, arms, hands, and fingers. Conclude by feeling your mouth, nose, cheeks, eyes, ears, forehead, and scalp.

This whole practice need not take more than a minute. But by its end you'll be back in your body, back in the moment, and able to bring a calmer, clearer perspective to the difficult situation at hand.

PUSH YOURSELF

Potential exists in every moment. Just beyond the boundaries of who we think we are and what we're capable of is always the potential for a new and surprising accomplishment. In order to achieve it, we need to let go of the usual and customary. We need to stretch our limits, gently, to become more of who we're meant to be.

The Practice:

Pick an arena of your life where you recognize the presence of clear limits. Such a limit might be a diet or exercise habit that you haven't been able to break. It might be a knee-jerk way that you express yourself or hide your true feelings. You also might be limited in how long you're able to stay present when faced with difficult emotions, or in your ability to treat yourself in a nurturing way.

Once you've selected the arena, zero in on a limit that you're willing to stretch over the next week. Think of executing this stretch as you would a yoga position—slowly and gradually exceeding your previous stopping point but never pushing beyond what you can safely maintain. In a very real way, if you commit yourself to this practice, you'll be a different person by the time it's complete.

WHOLE-BODY BREATHING

Expand, contract. It's the way of the universe, of all things, and certainly of the human body. Expanding and contracting freely with whole-body breathing allows us a great opportunity to sensitize ourselves to this eternal back-and-forth.

The Practice:

Lie down on a hard surface. Support your head with a pillow, and your knees as well if necessary. Breathe consciously, in an unforced rhythm, for about five minutes. With each inhale, imagine your breath spreading through your trunk and outward to all your extremities. See if you can experience a gentle inflating of even your fingers and toes. Let this whole-body breath fill you with energy and positive spirit.

GET CURIOUS

Curiosity is a major ally of presence. It engages us with the surrounding world and keeps our perspective constantly evolving. Plus, the act of discovery is often a sheer joy.

The Practice:

Pick a topic about which you'd like to know more and research it. Continue your exploration through travel. Start a conversation you wouldn't normally have. Involve your senses. Make a complete experience out of it. Don't stop until you've become even more curious than you were at the beginning.

INTENTIONAL DREAMING

Dreams usually provide more questions than they do answers. Are they a stress response? A secret code? A window to another world? There's one way, frequently unacknowledged, to penetrate this puzzle. Through the process of intentional dreaming, we can bring our conscious and unconscious minds together. The result creates not only an expansive sense of presence, but also powerful inner guidance.

The Practice:

For one week, keep a notebook by your bed. Each night, before going to sleep, think about an aspect of your life in which you'd like some guidance. Then ask your unconscious to provide you with a dream about that topic, and to make it one that you'll remember. If you wake up from a dream in the middle of the night, write it down before returning to sleep. If you recall it in the morning, make sure to write it down before beginning your day.

THE IN-BETWEEN STATE

We spend two thirds of our lives awake yet tuned into only a small sliver of what life has to offer. We spend almost one third of our lives asleep, unaware of anything whatsoever. Twice a day, however, we have an opportunity to leave our usual modes of existence and taste something altogether different. In the slippery moments between sleeping and waking lie altered states of consciousness that can help us break free of even the most oppressive limitations.

The Practice:

For one week, pay unusually close attention to what happens in the moments just before you drift off to sleep and just after you wake up the next morning. If possible, allow a little extra time before you open your eyes and arise fully.

During these in-between states, surrender to the strange mixture of thoughts, feelings, dreamy stories, and strange images that may arise. At the same time, don't lose your thread of awareness. Observe everything like a scientist, passionately curious but entirely nonjudgmental. Then, throughout the rest of the day, see if recalling this in-between state adds a new dimension or perspective to your ordinary consciousness.

SELF-ACUPRESSURE

Acupuncture, along with its no-needles offshoot, acupressure, works according to an energy-mapping system of the body that's thousands of years old. In the debate about how effectively this system stops pain and cures illness, what's often lost is that each person's response to it is unique and unpredictable. With a mindset combining open-ness and skepticism, always a potent duo for increasing presence, try this acupressure experiment the next time you're distracted or unfocused.

The Practice:

Hold your hand palm upward. Using the flat end of a pencil or pen, apply gentle and consistent pressure for five minutes to the indentation just above your wristbone and exactly in line with your pinky. In addition to providing mental clarity, this point, known as SI-5, is also said to help with decision-making. Try it a few times under different circumstances, and then keep it in your personal "toolbox" if you notice a benefit.

BESTOW GRATITUDE

In the words of William Blake, "Gratitude is heaven itself." Just the experience of feeling grateful (page 15) can connect us to a level of loving presence that's as warm and soothing as it is profound. But the bestowing of gratitude is even more heavenly. It creates a feedback loop of joy that keeps increasing as long as you let it.

The Practice:

Think of one or more people for whom you're deeply grateful. Be specific about why they inspire your gratitude. Once you've allowed yourself to exult in that gratitude, go ahead and share it. Don't ask for anything in return from those you thank, except that they receive your offering.

CONSCIOUS EATING

How many times have you craved one of your favorite foods, waited all day till you could have it, and then experienced no real enjoyment because your mind began wandering even before the first bite? Such "absent eating" is the norm, but it doesn't have to be.

The Practice:

For a week, stay entirely focused on the experience of eating through at least part of each meal. This includes smelling, tasting, savoring, chewing, swallowing, and pausing between bites. When your mind drifts, as it inevitably will, avoid any self-criticism and just gently return your focus to the food in front of you.

CHANGE A ROUTINE

Whenever we do something the same way, over and over, it tends to become rote. This bars us from the potential liveliness in the activity, as well as from the moment in which it's happening. Even a slight shift in the way we perform activities can snap us to attention. With more attention comes renewed presence, along with the fulfillment that presence always brings.

The Practice:

Pick a daily routine—perhaps your morning stretch, your route to work, or the way you brush your teeth. For the next few days, make a conscious choice to change one part of that routine. You might squeeze the toothpaste with your other hand, for instance, or reverse your usual order of brushing. Make the change something that requires your full attention, and make it different every day. Does the activity become more interesting? More pleasant?

A DAY OF SILENCE

Noise is everywhere. Much of our energy is unconsciously involved in filtering out noises we don't want to hear. On top of those noises, we often layer ones we do want to hear—radio, TV, music, conversation. All that noise can bar us from a direct connection to the present moment. Plus, all this external noise tends to feed the incessant chatter within our minds. There is no better tonic for our jangled and distracted lives, therefore, than the periodic invocation of silence.

The Practice:

Choose a day when you don't have to work and when you can count on the support of those around you. Designate this day as one of complete silence. This means not uttering a single word from the time you awaken till the time you go to sleep. In addition, make it a point not to turn on or use any nonessential noise-making devices. Left with the sounds of nature and a bit of white noise, let this day be a Sabbath of sorts, reintroducing you to your quieter, more essential self.

SEE THROUGH JUDGMENTS

A judgment is always subjective. That means it's not verifiably true or false. Yet judgments carry an enormous amount of power, and the ones we make about ourselves are the most powerful of all. Seeing through such judgments, and their limitations, helps us to remain open, spontaneous, and capable of reaching our full potential.

The Practice:

List three of your best qualities. Then see if you can think of a circumstance in which each quality might become a hindrance. This might happen, perhaps, if the quality were applied inappropriately or in an exaggerated fashion. Suppose that you're deliberate, for example. Too much deliberation might cause you to miss an important opportunity that requires swift action.

Now list three of your worst qualities. See if you can think of a circumstance in which each quality might actually become beneficial. A quick temper, for example, might keep you from bottling up your feelings.

If you can't come up with answers to either part of this practice, ask someone to assist you. When finished, assess whether you now place even just a little less stock in your personal litany of self-judgments.

STANDING MEDITATION

Buddhist teacher Sylvia Boorstein wrote a book called Don't Just Do Something, Sit There. *The title alludes humorously to the way that constant doing prevents us from celebrating the present moment. Meditation is a well-known antidote to addictive doing. When most people think of meditation, they bring up images of people cross-legged on cushions. Meditation can be practiced in any position, however, and standing upright is one of the best.*

The Practice:

Stand up straight. Place your feet a comfortable distance apart. Let your hands fall in a relaxed and natural manner at your sides. Remain this way for fifteen minutes.

During this time, experiment with different types of focus. Begin by focusing on the feeling of your feet against the ground. Move on to the sights you're taking in, and then the sounds. Focus on your breathing for a while, and then on any other sensations arising in your body. If you feel pain, don't resist it. Whenever your mind wanders, gently bring it back to your current mode of focus. Conclude the meditation by following the unimpeded flow of your awareness as it flits from within you to without you, and from one passing phenomenon to the next.

NIGHT SKY

In Cloud Figures (PAGE 30), *you gave yourself a leisurely chance to lie outside and gaze upward. Now it's time to reprise that practice, but in the wee small hours. There's an aspect of being that comes out only at night, when we're able to place our usually overwhelming human dramas in the context of an infinite universe.*

The Practice:

Choose a clear, starry night and an hour when most of the world is fast asleep. Make sure you're warm and comfortable as you lie on your back and watch the dark sky shimmer and twinkle. Use this practice to contemplate the enormity of existence and the eons of time that have passed and are yet to come. From the vantage point of this truly universal perspective, what does the present moment feel like? How does this moment inform or enlighten the ones in your everyday schedule?

SPIN

Have you ever seen a whirling dervish? Have you ever wondered about the purpose of the dance? Dervishes, from the same Sufi sect as the great mystical poet Rumi, use the spinning ceremony as a meditation in movement. They aim to become a sacred axis, integrating all realms of being—physical, emotional, mental, and spiritual.

The Practice:

Even apart from the intricate Sufi ritual, spinning can yield similar effects. Begin with silence or slow, lilting music. Keep one leg in place and rotate around it with the other. Stretch your arms almost all the way outward, using them to help propel yourself. Hold your head upright and your gaze level. Spin this way for a couple of minutes. If you get dizzy, pause for a moment and then resume, moving a little slower than before.

When you're ready, experiment with a faster pace and a change of direction. Make the movement your own, remaining as present as possible to the flow of each spin and to the sensation it evokes. No matter your speed, the more present you are, the less dizzy you'll become. In time, the spin may take on a life of its own.

REFINE YOUR FRIENDSHIPS

Friendships are easier to begin than they are to end. No ritual, like divorce, marks their conclusion. Therefore, we often remain in friendships long after they have ceased to serve us or to reflect who we've grown to be. That's why it's helpful to periodically let some friendships go and to inject an entirely new spirit into others.

The Practice:

Make a list of the ten friends with whom you spend the most time. Put a check mark beside the name of anyone who truly knows, sees, and loves the person you are right now. One by one, consider the relationships that didn't earn this distinction. Decide whether it's time to let them go or to begin an overhaul.

If you need to let a friendship go, allow yourself to feel all the emotions that this decision might bring up. Then, when you're clear and open, proceed in the most loving way possible. If you need to overhaul a friendship, follow the same process. In both situations, be ready for your friends to surprise you. Some might not be up to the challenge that such a moment of truth provides, while others might show new, beautiful colors.

TRACE THE SOURCE

Contemporary life comes processed, packaged, and ready to consume. Rarely do we pay heed to the natural sources of things or to the thousands of people involved in creating and delivering all our conveniences. Even though most of this process is invisible to us, it's a vital part of what's happening in each and every moment. Becoming more conscious of where things come from and how they get here is a simple way to honor the entire web of being.

The Practice:

Try this practice first in your living room, then your bedroom, and finally your kitchen. Begin by scanning your surroundings for all the elements present: for example, the walls, paint, flooring, furniture, textiles, appliances, and all the remaining objects, whether functional, aesthetic, or edible.

For each element you find, consider what it's made of and where that substance originated. Think about how the substance was extracted, refined, and shaped into its current form. Try to identify all the individuals who played a role in bringing the object to you, such as laborers, managers, salespeople, and distributors. Your private abode is truly a global project—are you changed in any way by this discovery?

TOY TIME

Remember the Slinky? Pick-Up Sticks? Jacks? Legos? The toys you loved most as a child provided countless hours of enraptured contentment. Until the call came for dinner or bedtime, you wanted nothing else but to be where you were, doing exactly what you were doing. You were an ace at the how of now without even knowing it. The good news is that no matter how many years have passed, those favorite toys can still work their very same magic.

The Practice:

If you don't still own some great classic toys, take a trip to the store and stock up. The best ones often cost the least. When you're ready, set aside an hour with no clocks, no distractions, and no to-do lists. Allow the toy to pull you into its lyrical realm. Revel in any memories that arise, yet remain mindful of your connection to the present.

If you're tempted to spend toy time with a child, go ahead, but only if you can avoid falling into the grown-up role. Just for this hour, let there be no grown-ups anywhere in sight.

GIVE YOURSELF A MASSAGE

While most of us are familiar with the benefits of loving touch—stroking, cuddling, massaging—we rarely think of touching ourselves in such a manner. Sensual self-contact, however, fosters openness and receptivity. It creates a relationship to the present moment that's tactile, playful, and soft.

The Practice:

After bathing, rub yourself gently from head to toe. If you like, use some lotion or oil. Don't massage with a purpose, such as releasing tension or loosening muscles, but rather for the sheer pleasure of it. Feel the parts of your body that most often go untouched. Continue massaging until your whole body silently says, "Yum."

TAKE THE OPPOSITE SIDE

The more forcefully we cling to our opinions, the more narrow our perspective becomes. That's why it's so valuable, every once in a while, to refresh our viewpoint by stepping far away from it.

The Practice:

Select a subject about which you have a passionate opinion. Then, gather as much information as possible in support of the opposing side and try to find merit in it. When you're finished, notice whether your position on the subject is now a little broader in perspective.

PITCH DARK

One of the biggest detractors from presence is fear. Or, more precisely, our relationship with fear. In the face of fear, we usually shut down, lose our connection to ourselves and the present moment. But it's equally possible to embrace *the experience of fear, to move through its rise and release, and to learn what's on the other side.*

The Practice:

Find the nearest place that, when not illuminated, is pitch dark. Make sure that the site you choose is not actually dangerous, and bring a flashlight. Once you're there, extinguish any lights that are on, including the flashlight. Remain in the total darkness, if you can, for at least a minute. Feel any and all sensations that arise, especially fear. Become a student of your fear. Where does it reside in your body? What does it do to your breath? Does it intensify with time? Does it ever diminish, even for a moment?

When the minute has passed, temporarily turn on the flashlight to take a break. Then, when you're ready, resume the practice a few more times, persevering in the darkness a little longer with each repetition.

CRAWL

We like to think that we grow more aware with age, but it's a myth. What actually happens is that we become more aware of certain things and less aware of others. Each stage of life has its own presence, wisdom, and power. Before we learn to walk, our all-fours perspective on the world creates unique relationships to people, creatures, and objects. This perspective soon disappears from our lives forever—until we're willing to spend a few minutes reclaiming it.

The Practice:

Get on your hands and knees and crawl around. That's really all there is to it. Try this practice at home, making sure to visit all your usual spots. Notice how they differ when seen from this vantage point. In addition, gravitate to any nooks and crannies that usually elude you while you're standing, sitting, or walking but that now call your attention. If there are adults, kids, and pets around, all the better. Let yourself laugh and feel silly and helpless. Most of all, keep your mind tilted toward any experience or input that's available only at ground level.

THE PRESENCE PRAYER

There are many types of prayer. Most of us grew up learning about petitionary prayer, wherein we ask the God in which we believe for something in particular. But prayer does not require a belief in God, nor does it necessitate any outward focus. With the Presence Prayer, we simply reinforce our intent to be present, and then allow guidance in that quest to emerge from within. Amazingly, it almost always does.

The Practice:

Set aside fifteen minutes and retreat to a quiet place. Choose any comfortable position. Settle into a breathing pattern that is calm and unforced. Then silently ask the following question: *What aspect of my life is calling for further presence?*

Once the question has been asked, turn your attention inward and wait patiently for the answer to emerge. It might be about anything at all—emotions, relationships, health, work. When the answer comes, let it reverberate for a while. See what other information comes along with it. Perhaps you were previously avoiding this information, or maybe it was lurking on the fringes of your awareness. Now that it's out in the open, use this prayerful moment to embrace it completely.

DIALOGUE WITH YOUR DISTRESS

As soon as we become upset about something, our minds shift into overdrive. They want to understand the situation, get control over it, and figure out the best possible resolution. The mind usually doesn't realize, or like to admit, that all the information necessary to resolve most distress is already present. In order to access this information, we just need to tune in.

The Practice:

Distress, in this context, means anything at all that's causing you to feel bad. It could be a headache, an insult, or a fight with a friend. The next time you're feeling bad, catch yourself before you launch into a mental dissection of the situation. Instead, notice exactly where you feel the distress in your body. Maintain a gentle focus on the distress until you're fully connected to it.

Next, silently ask the distress two questions: (1) *What's really the matter?* (2) *What do you need from me in regard to this problem?*

Be patient with your inquiry, as if you were asking the questions of a bright but distraught child. On rare occasions, when the answers arrive they will suggest a complete and satisfactory course of action. Most of the time, at the very least, they'll provide you with invaluable insights.

TOTAL REPOSE

Much of the tension in our bodies goes unnoticed, lurking just beyond our awareness as a vague sense of discomfort. Becoming conscious of such tension provides us with a simple and relaxing way to release it.

The Practice:

Lie down on a hard surface. Support your head with a pillow, and your knees as well if necessary. Let yourself sink into the surface completely, as in the corpse pose in yoga.

Beginning at your toes, perform a slow and steady body scan. Include every part of your body. Whenever you encounter an area that's completely relaxed, bask in that relaxation. Whenever you find some tension, pause for a moment. Don't stress or fight it. Just keep your attention focused specifically on that spot for the next few breaths. Imagine all that tension melting away. Even if it doesn't melt completely, you've definitely begun the process.

MINE YOUR MEMORIES

Out of the millions of moments that make up our lives, we actually remember very few. Those that we do remember, therefore, are often distorted. They can seem more intense or important than the original experience. Strung together, these moments make up the stories of our lives. We tell these stories often, to ourselves and to others, believing that they're entirely true. When we narrow our past in such a way, we also narrow our availability to the present. Things that don't fit our ongoing stories are often ignored or not even noticed. Mining for buried memories keeps us open, aware, and ready for brand-new experience.

The Practice:

Pick a major memory from your early past. Let the usual thoughts and images associated with it float to the surface of your awareness. Instead of stopping there, as usual, keep focusing on that time until related memories arise. Do they change the meaning of that event at all? Do they alter its flavor? If it's a good memory, can you find anything about it that wasn't so good? If it's a bad memory, can you find anything about it that wasn't so bad?

BLOW BUBBLES

Sometimes, when we're shut down by stress or overwhelmed, all it takes to restore our flow is a momentary vacation.

The Practice:

Buy a jar of bubble solution. Blow bubbles for five minutes. Make it a meditation, staying playfully absorbed as you dip the wand, stretch the bubbles into existence with your breath, and then watch their journeys until they are no more.

EMBRACE A TREE

Notice that the name of this celebration avoids the word hug*? That's because* tree hugger *has become a misleading insult referring to environmentalists. The act of putting your arms around a tree, however, has nothing to do with that cliché. It's a simple, powerful, and delightful way to connect with the awesome energy of nature.*

The Practice:

Find a time and a place at which you can do this privately and therefore avoid any self-consciousness. Maintain this position for a few minutes, breathing, listening, sensing, until there's no longer a distinct you and a distinct tree—just the unifying experience of the embrace.

A DAY WITHOUT TIME

Jerry Seinfeld used to joke that, when dealing with TV and the remote control, women want to know what's on, while men want to know what else is on. When it comes to the subject of time, however, there is no gender gap. Often, both men and women have less interest in what's happening now than in what's happening next. We all constantly glance at the clock or our watches, habitually keeping an eye fixed on the future. Eliminating our access to timepieces, even for a short while, can help us to appreciate each passing moment.

The Practice:

For one twenty-four hour period, put away all watches and cover all clocks. Try to avoid any location where you'll accidentally run into either. Steer clear of activities, or media, that occur on a familiar schedule. If you feel compelled to know where you are in the cycle of the day, check the position of the sun or the moon. In addition, whenever that compulsion arises, let it be a call to the Now. Notice what you feel in your body, the quality of your thoughts, and everything that's present in your surroundings.

ACTING OUT

The people who bother us most often reflect aspects of ourselves that we haven't yet allowed into our present-moment awareness. These aspects reside in what psychologists refer to as the "shadow." Pretending to be the people who bother us, and acting out those people's worst qualities, is a powerful way to bring what's in shadow to light.

The Practice:

Pick someone who really bugs you, who has a behavior so annoying that it makes you cringe. Now act out this person's behavior. Don't just make a timid attempt—exaggerate the quality until you can really *feel* it. Continue acting this way for at least a few minutes. When you're done, investigate whether even a trace of this annoying quality exists in yourself. If so, are you willing to accept it? Keep in mind that complete acceptance is always the first step toward positive change.

PLANT SOMETHING

In every moment there is birth, growth, decline, and death. This cycle plays out on levels from the molecular to the universal. Within a human life, it transpires physically, emotionally, mentally, and spiritually. Shepherding this cycle for another life form helps us attune ourselves to its constant presence.

The Practice:

Purchase a packet of seeds for a plant you'd like to grow. Choose a plant that's either annual or perennial so you can experience all aspects of its life cycle within the passage of a few seasons. Follow the directions for planting and tending it. View the plant for at least a minute once or twice a week. If the plant survives, watch for times of steady progression, plateaus, and sudden spurts of growth. If the plant doesn't make it, try to determine what was responsible for its demise. Then plant another seed and do your best to help it thrive.

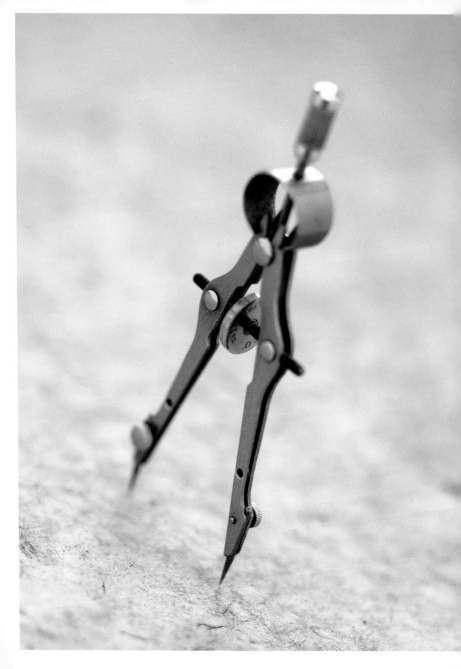

PROCLAIM YOUR NAME

There's an aspect of being that exists at a deeper level than any of the roles we assume in everyday life. It's beyond what we think, feel, say, or do. This state of consciousness is often referred to in spiritual traditions as the "I Am." Understanding the "I Am" is helpful—experiencing it directly *can be truly profound.*

The Practice:

Find a location where no one can hear you. Speak your name slowly, at normal volume, articulating each syllable separately and clearly. Do this ten times. Next, proclaim your name as loudly as possible, in a voice midway between speaking and singing. Draw out each syllable even longer than before.

How does that feel? Can you fully claim the "I Am" for yourself, or do you shrink from it? Continue proclaiming your name until you feel spacious, energized, and powerful. For added effect, do this practice with a supportive friend. Let the presence of a witness intensify, and then break through, any lingering doubt about the spirit at your core.

ACTIVE LISTENING

Often, in conversation, we don't pay very close attention. Before the other person is even halfway through making a point, we're already rehearsing our rebuttal or commiseration. Even more frequently, we're lost in thought about something in our own experience that's related to the conversation's topic. In the process, we lose our connection to our conversation partner and to the present moment as well. One way to quickly restore those connections is the practice of active listening.

The Practice:

This is a two-day practice. On the first day, simply observe yourself closely during conversations. Notice when you're fully present and when you check out. Watch for both physical and mental fidgeting. See how frequently you go off on an internal tangent while the other person is still speaking.

On the second day, each time a conversation partner shares something important, summarize its content and ask whether you understand it correctly. If you don't, ask to hear it again and then revise your summary. Resist all urges to focus the conversation on yourself. Watch for any effect this practice has on the *quality* of each discussion.

RIVER OF WORDS

As anyone who keeps a journal knows, the act of writing is a revelation. We often start out saying one thing and end up on an entirely different subject. In the process, our words reveal previously hidden aspects of ourselves. To make the most of this opportunity, it's vital not to edit our words or pause at all between them. What often appears, in the river of words, are the deepest aspects of who we are right now.

The Practice:

Choose a pen and notebook that appeal to your senses, or use a computer if you prefer the speed that a keyboard provides. Either way, begin by focusing your mind on this question: *What is the most important truth about my life right now that I need to face and explore?*

Write for ten minutes without stopping. Don't lift your pen from the page or your fingers from the keyboard. If words don't seem to come, write about how hard it is to get going. No matter what, keep writing. Soon the river of words will begin to flow, and so will your self-discovery.

TRANSCEND YOUR STYLE

Style exists not just in the realm of fashion but in every aspect of life. We have styles of speech, behavior, work, sex, and even religion. Wherever there is style, there is also division. It's a basic human trait to align with those who share our style and to oppose, even if subtly, those who don't. This keeps us from the radical openness and acceptance that full presence requires. Surrendering even one aspect of our style is a powerful inducement to break free from this limitation.

The Practice:

Think a bit about your style. What kind of clothes, music, film, culture, and subculture do you and your friends prefer? Next make a list of what you consider to be significant stylistic faux pas, such as big hair, violent action flicks, junk food, or tie-dye. Then choose something from the list and indulge in it. Tease your hair, for example, or sit through the last movie you'd ever want to watch. Go totally against your grain. In the process, see if you can find something in common with those who prefer this style. Don't conclude the practice until you can enjoy, even a little, your temporary transgression.

SELF-INQUIRY

A great sage in India, Ramana Maharshi, wanted to help his disciples break through all illusions of the ego. He sought to provide them with experiential proof that they were each indivisible from all of creation and that any sense of personal separation was totally false. Every moment, according to Ramana, was a sacred whole. He believed that all we need to do to realize these truths is to undertake a simple, yet profound, form of self-inquiry.

The Practice:

Growing up, you became accustomed to saying "I" to describe yourself. But of what is this "I" composed? Where do you find it? And how? These are the questions that self-inquiry poses.

To practice it and find your own answers, begin to track down the "I" whenever it seems to appear. When a thought arises, ask yourself, *Am I this thought?* When a feeling arises, ask yourself, *Am I this feeling?* Ask the same thing with each and every sensation and experience you have. If you encounter a self that seems to separately witness all of the above, ask yourself, *Am I this witness?* Keep probing deeper and deeper to find your absolute essence. Do you feel part of a sacred whole?

SET A TIMER

When growing our muscle of present-moment awareness, it's helpful to have periodic reminders. A reminder can call us back to attention whenever we're distracted or in a fit of reaction. Sometimes just a one-second beep can prevent us from spinning out completely.

The Practice:

Program your watch or cell phone to beep every five, ten, fifteen, or twenty minutes. Whenever you hear the beep, stop what you're doing for a moment and ask yourself: *Am I present? What am I feeling in my body? Is there anything at all I'm resisting? What else is happening right now?*

BLINDFOLD

Sight, for most people, is the dominant sense. Our reliance on vision, critical though it is, often precludes us from experiencing more of what's happening in any given moment. Temporarily denying ourselves the blessing of sight can create a new appreciation for it, and in the process sharpen all our other senses.

The Practice:

Spend an hour at home wearing a blindfold that totally blocks your vision. Allow yourself time to become comfortable with any disorientation that might occur. Then go about your usual business—phone calls, grooming, chores, gardening—and see how much you can actually accomplish. Notice whether you become more aware of sounds, smells, or the feel of things.

DEATH REHEARSAL

When will you die? Thirty years from now? Ten years? Tomorrow? The fact is, no one can know the answer to this question. Yet many of us live as if we've got all the time in the world. We put off what really matters and instead focus on trivial things. Accepting death's shadow, by contrast, can quickly snap us out of this habit. In a strange paradox, the more we embrace the ever-present possibility of death, the more we come to life.

The Practice:

Part one: For five minutes, imagine that you're going to die in a month. Picture the process as being fast and painless but irreversible. No more ripe Bing cherries, laughing babies, swoons of love, or ocean walks. Sink into the sense that everything in your existence will be gone.

Part two: Flush with the sense of this imaginary demise, make a list of the ten most important things to do before the day arrives. The list can include anything from "See Kathmandu" to "Forgive my father" to "Stop caring about what other people think." Next, with the knowledge that you might live for decades or only days, schedule every single item on your list.

INCREASE YOUR GRATITUDE

The depth of our gratitude parallels the depth of our presence. Cultivate Gratitude (PAGE 15) *and* Bestow Gratitude (PAGE 59) *described two ways to deepen both. In addition to these methods, there's one more. Finding reasons to be grateful in the worst possible situations is an advanced practice that yields lifelong benefits.*

The Practice:

Think of the three worst things that ever happened to you. Consider whether something you are grateful for arose out of each calamity. The death of a loved one, for instance, can break your heart. But a broken heart, in turn, can make you more accepting and tolerant of others.

If you're unable to find a silver lining of gratitude regarding one or more of your difficult passages, let the question live in you for a few weeks. Sometimes the most important answer appears when we're not even consciously looking for it.

SEE THE CHILD

One of the least acknowledged aspects of our lives is how emotionally vulnerable we all are. Beneath even the thickest skin huddles a sensitive soul—otherwise why would such skin be necessary? We pretend to be tough and then mistakenly assume that everyone else is, too. Yet by recognizing our shared vulnerability, we can put an end to all that. In place of denial, we're able to bring an authentic, healing awareness to what transpires behind our protective facades.

The Practice:

Remember what it was like to be seven years old? Remember how easy it was to get your feelings hurt? Remember how every little tease, slight, or dirty look could send you into a fit of tears or rage or petulant withdrawal?

For the next week, during all your interactions with adults, picture them as seven-year-old children. Treat them, whether complete strangers or the closest of friends, with the same attentive caring that you craved at that age. Watch how it makes everyone around you feel, and how it makes you feel as well.

BEFRIEND YOUR PAIN

Whenever we feel physical pain, our instinctive response is a whole-body flinch. We immediately gird ourselves against the pain in order to get rid of it, which often prolongs and intensifies the pain instead. Eventually, the effects of such a flinch can become worse than the pain itself. The opposite approach—befriending the pain—might seem like choosing to suffer. Actually, it's a rare form of presence that almost always leads to significant relief.

The Practice:

Reserve this practice for the next time you have a headache, muscle ache, or similar bodily pain. Begin when you become aware of your flinch, both its physical aspects and any thought patterns that arise. Gently relax your body as much as possible, and then place your focus directly at the center of the pain. Breathe into it over and over, noticing everything you can about the pain.

Is it hot or cold? Sharp or dull? Does it stay steady or fluctuate? Is a shape or color associated with it? What else does it communicate to you? Continue breathing into the pain and noticing everything about it until it departs completely or becomes more tolerable.

BEFRIEND YOUR PAIN (REVISITED)

Just like physical pain, emotional pain resides in the body. There's nowhere else we ever feel it. But most of the time, we feel it for only a few moments before reverting to the same kind of flinch that physical pain evokes. An emotional flinch differs from a physical flinch in one key way, however. It usually lodges somewhere specific—the gut, chest, shoulders, neck, temples—and traps the pain inside. Befriending emotional pain requires that we first access the flinch, which then allows the stuck emotion to release. Such a release, though it's often intense, is almost always incredibly freeing.

The Practice:

The next time you feel a constriction in any part of your body and have an inkling that it's emotion-related, gently place your attention at that location. Don't try to change or understand the sensation. Just let it be exactly as it is. Soon this acceptance will allow the constriction to release. Then you'll be face to face with the emotion it temporarily blocked. Keep your attention on this emotion as it wells up and begins to move through you. Is it easier to feel than you imagined? Do you prefer this feeling to remaining shut down?

CHANT

For centuries, people have used repetitive sound as a way to expand their awareness of the Now, and particularly to access its subtle and extraordinary dimensions. Usually, this chanting has taken place within a religious context. All its benefits, however, are available in any context whatsoever.

The Practice:

Find a location where no one can hear you. Warm up by choosing a one-syllable word. This word could be anything from "Om" to "Peace" to "Yes." Chant this word for one minute, without varying your pace, volume, or intonation.

Continue for ten minutes more. Stay with your original chant, if you like, or switch to a longer phrase that works for you. Some people enjoy "May all beings be happy," for example, while others prefer chants from ancient Hebrew, Sanskrit, Arabic, or Tibetan. It's also possible to select a series of sounds with no meaning at all.

Whenever your mind drifts off, gently bring it back to the sound and the rhythm of your chant. Take special note of any unusual feelings or sensations that arise.

SERVE YOUR COMMUNITY

The usual pitch, when it comes to volunteering, is that it's appropriate to give something back. We're called upon to serve as a fundamental responsibility. What this pitch obscures is that service is actually a privilege. Whether in a soup kitchen, battered-women's shelter, or Little League, service opens our hearts, connects us to the world, and fills the present moment with meaning. While service often provides great assistance to those in need, its foremost beneficiary is almost always the one who serves.

The Practice:

Find a few hours a week for service. Choose a location or organization that you feel strongly about. Look for a position that takes advantage of your strengths or one that involves a refreshing change of pace from your usual work. Since the opportunity to make a contribution is a privilege, treat everyone you meet with appreciation.

FINGER PAINT

Do you remember finger painting in preschool or kindergarten? There were no rules, no self-consciousness, no approval to seek or anything to achieve. Instead, it was a time to revel, to make a tactile mess, and to watch with wide-eyed curiosity as the result took shape. Rare are the moments when we, as adults, grant ourselves such innocence and freedom. But when we do, they can joyously bring us back to life.

The Practice:

Find a big piece of paper or cardboard. It doesn't have to be new or designed for this purpose—anything out of the recycle bin will do. Now choose your "paint." If you've got actual finger paint around, use it. If not, make ridiculous concoctions out of whatever's around—coffee, juice, food coloring, lipstick, lotion. You might even want to get out the blender. When you're ready to paint, don't try to create an actual image. Let your masterpiece be goopy, swirly, a dramatic Rorschach of your inner life right now.

EARS WIDE OPEN

Color Scan (PAGE 26), One-Minute Body Merge (PAGE 51), *and* Blow Bubbles (PAGE 80), *are three ways to come back to the present moment when you're stressed, anxious, or distracted. One more method of reconnection involves acutely tuning into sound. Few things are as effective as the raw, direct experience of sound in helping you to become calm, centered, and alert.*

The Practice:

Whenever you leave the present moment, you might feel tense, spacey, numb, or some combination of the three. Once you recognize that this has occurred, stop what you're doing as soon as possible. Stand or sit perfectly still. Close your eyes.

Now listen intently to every sound around you. These might include birds, wind, traffic, conversation, media, appliance white noise, or even sounds you're unable to identify. What's important is to register each sound one by one, let it penetrate you fully, and then widen your focus until another sound appears. Continue this practice for as long as it takes to fully orient yourself in time and space.

ASK AWAY

Get Curious (PAGE 54) *suggested learning more about something that intrigues you. Now it's time to learn more about a person in your life. Whether casual acquaintances or intimate partners, other people are always much more complex and engaging than we tend to think. Often, we get used to them as they appear to be and then stop inquiring. The act of inquiry, especially when it involves what we assume we already know, can bring surprising depth to our interactions.*

The Practice:

At a time when there's no stress or other topic on your agenda, tell a few people in your life that you want to know a little more about them. Explain that your purpose is simply to learn and understand. Beforehand, make sure to think of a few ideas about what direction to explore with your questions. If the first question doesn't get the conversation flowing, move on.

Generally, people love it when others take a real interest in them. Most likely, you'll be pleased at how easy this practice is and how much surprising information it reveals.

TONGLEN

The news of the world, with all its dissension and strife, causes many of us to feel helpless. We turn away from what's happening both down the block and around the globe. In so doing we deny our role in world events and limit our capacity to serve as a healing force. The Tibetan practice of Tonglen is a simple, lovely way to prevent this process.

The Practice:

Whenever you see someone suffering, notice whether it causes you to flinch, go numb, or shut down in any way. If so, this is a perfect opportunity for Tonglen. Here's how it works. With the power of your imagination, take all the pain that you've witnessed directly into your heart. Behold that pain with compassion and empathy, transmuting it into love. Once this is complete, send all that love back to the original sufferer.

Tonglen allows you to remain connected to the world during even the most troubled times. This connection, in turn, may inspire you to become further involved. Once you're familiar with it, try making Tonglen your customary response to bad news, even before any shutdown occurs.

BE PASSIONATELY AVERAGE

Striving for excellence is how we change, grow, and reach our full potential. But since we can't excel at everything, it's also how we become self-critical and perfectionistic. Urging ourselves toward unreachable perfection robs us of the ease and spontaneity that are hallmarks of the Now. But exulting in activities we enjoy, with no intention of great achievement, is a foolproof perfectionist's cure.

The Practice:

Are there pursuits you enjoy but can't do well? Or ones that you think you'd enjoy but avoid due to lack of aptitude? Pick one or two and pursue them with complete gusto. Perhaps this means salsa dancing with two left feet, knitting sweaters with lopsided patterns, or bowling a record-setting series of gutter balls. Whatever the pursuit, perform it with the intention of celebrating your mediocrity rather than cringing at it. If and when a cringe does occur, just laugh yourself through it and keep going. If possible judgment by others makes this practice too daunting, do it with a friend who's willing to be just as goofily gung-ho.

RECONNECT WITH SOMEONE YOU LOVE

In every life, the quickly passing tide of events leaves a number of friendships in its wake. Some are best left behind, as discussed in **Refine Your Friendships** (PAGE 67), *because they draw upon aspects of ourselves that aren't healthy or no longer fit the people we've since become. But other friendships slipped away for no real reason, taking important parts of ourselves with them. Reconnecting with such friends is a beautiful way to enrich the Now.*

The Practice:

Reminisce about your friends from childhood, adolescence, and the years since. Inevitably, if you give it enough time, your mind will land upon some people with whom you inadvertently lost touch. Think about each of these people individually, noticing which one touches your heart most. Then track that person down, finding a phone number or an email or postal address. When you're ready, reconnect. If reconnecting feels as good as you imagined, invite this person to renew the friendship.

MIRROR GAZING

As the adage says, "The eyes are the mirror of the soul." Looking into a pair of eyes can transport us to dimensions of presence and spirit like nothing else. This is especially true of looking into our own eyes, which is why the ancient practice of mirror gazing can often be surprisingly potent.

The Practice:

Sit or stand comfortably within one foot of a mirror. Gaze at your own eyes for at least ten minutes. Allow your focus to be soft but steady. If you experience the temptation to look away, try your best to resist it.

What do you see? Does your face "shape-shift"? Does your image begin to disappear? Whatever happens, note it calmly and without undue fascination. And if nothing out of the ordinary happens, use the time, and the unusual circumstance, to pay close attention to your feelings, thoughts, and sensations.

·

DE-AGGRAVATE

The world is full of things that aggravate us—bad drivers, long lines, corruption, poverty, people who are rude, greedy, or passive-aggressive. Every time we encounter such aggravations, they shut us down and bar us from the present moment. While we think it's external experiences themselves that are so unbearable, it's actually the internal *emotions they evoke. Discovering these emotions, and finally feeling them, can defuse even our biggest aggravations.*

The Practice:

Select three life experiences that tend to aggravate you most. Conjure each one, let it live in you for a while, and pay close attention to exactly how it makes you feel. A controlling person, for example, might make you feel powerless. In most cases, the emotion you uncover will be among the most difficult for you to feel. Feeling it during this practice, and again whenever it arises in the future, will gradually make experiencing it much easier. That's why, seen from this perspective, aggravations are such a gift. They're like flashing neon arrows pointing at the precise places you most need to open.

PRETEND TO TANGO

Be Moved (PAGE 39) *described a way to become more fully present by connecting with rhythms outside ourselves. While that practice is performed solo, this one produces a similar result in union with another person. The art of the tango relies upon exquisite awareness of the subtlest energies passing between partners. Even if you don't know the techniques of tango, it's possible to use it as a take-off point for a luscious impromptu duet.*

The Practice:

Select some sultry music that appeals to both you and your partner. As you begin moving together to the music, imagine that there's a magnetic force between the two of you. Tune into that force and let it be the source of your dance. Rather than moving separately from or in response to your partner, move only in unison.

Accomplishing this feat may seem challenging, especially if you don't think of yourself as a dancer, but in reality it isn't. It relies—no surprise—on present-moment awareness. It builds upon and deepens that awareness. The goal is not expertise or even grace. All that matters is that you remain attuned to the flow.

ACKNOWLEDGE YOUR MULTIPLE PERSONALITIES

Most of us spend a tremendous amount of energy trying to be who we think we are, or should be. It's as if our vast and contradictory totality is supposed to cram itself into a straitjacket of sameness. A neat person can't tolerate moments of pure sloth. A garrulous person is confused when overcome with bouts of shyness. A prim person is horrified by depraved sexual fantasies. The truth is that we're all multiple personalities. Embracing our wide-ranging "selves" allows us to stay present no matter which ones or how many show up.

The Practice:

Draw a circle on a sheet of paper. Make a horizontal line through it. In the top half, write the names of some personalities you identify with most. These might include, for example, the Hard Worker, the Pleaser, or the Big Spender. In the bottom half, write the names of some personalities that you identify with least. Opposing the selves above, these might include the Goof-Off, the Narcissist, or the Tightwad. Keep this list with you for a week, making an effort to forge a closer relationship with those selves from the bottom half. Continue adding to both halves of the circle as new selves become apparent.

PENNILESS

It's often said that we're all just a few bad breaks away from dire poverty, but our lives rarely feel that way. The panhandler on the corner seems to reside in an entirely different universe. Our many creature comforts, however, obscure aspects of ourselves that otherwise we'd have to face. Stripping away some of those comforts, in a temporary yet dramatic fashion, can be as eye-opening as it is transformative.

The Practice:

For one day, when the circumstances of your life allow it, leave all your money and bank cards at home. Let yourself experience a taste of what it's like to be totally broke. No money for coffee, lunch, sundries, or whatever catches your eye.

Do you feel naked? Exposed? Vulnerable? If so, pay attention to your instinctive reactions to those feelings. Notice whether you relate differently to your coworkers. At some point, without revealing why, ask to borrow change from a person you don't know well. Do you feel embarrassed, perhaps, or ashamed?

When the day comes to a close, review what you've learned about yourself. Consider, in addition, whether pretending to be penniless will change the way you relate to those who are truly deprived.

DRUM

Like Chant (PAGE 97), *drumming is an ancient way to induce deep presence. The steady beat of a drum is a persistent call — "Wake up, wake up, wake up." But what are we waking up to? For some it's the rhythm that pulses through all of creation. For many it's the animal wildness that we often mask or deny. And for others, especially those burdened by stress and responsibility, it's the long-lost taste of freedom.*

The Practice:

If you have a drum, great. If not, find anything to beat upon that has a stirring sound. Begin with simple, repetitive patterns. Stick with each one long enough to feel it resonate within your body and become virtually self-propelling.

Then, over the next ten minutes, vary your drumming patterns to include different paces, volume levels, and degrees of complexity. Don't get caught up in a sense of performance or perfectionism. Instead, let your drumming be messy, surprising, and outrageous.

RESPECT YOUR WIRING

Some people are excitable, while others are placid. Some people excel at following directions, while others are best at improvising. Most of us spend a tremendous amount of our lives wishing that we were wired differently, that we could magically shift the basic aspects of our personalities at will. This creates self-opposition, which keeps us from being present to what is. Accepting something about ourselves that we've long resisted, by contrast, is a wonderful way to relax into the Now.

The Practice:

Select one aspect of your wiring that you consistently disdain. Perhaps you're shy or talk too much. Perhaps you tend to isolate yourself or to socialize compulsively. Whatever it is, give yourself a moment to stop fighting. Just let it be. You don't have to like it—just accept it. See how it feels to live without any opposition to this trait. Keep going until you're loose, expanded, and flowing with energy. Ironically, to whatever degree change is possible, this type of energy is exactly what will bring it about.

CRADLE THE BABY

Befriend Your Pain (Revisited) (PAGE 96) *described a way to create emotional release and freedom. This approach works beautifully with almost all painful emotions, but it requires an additional component when you're facing the most challenging types of hurt, loss, and disappointment. That's where cradling the baby comes in, a practice refined by Buddhist nun Yvonne Rand. It creates a powerful healing bond between the part of ourselves that feels the pain and the part that observes it.*

The Practice:

If you find yourself beset by a particularly difficult emotion, begin by opening to it as described in *Befriend Your Pain (Revisited)*. Once you're in direct contact with the emotion's physical presence, regard the sensation in the way a parent does a crying infant. Bring your attention close enough to the pain that it feels safe and nurtured, but not so close that it feels pressured in any way. Maintain this tender orientation to the pain until you become at least a little more calm and peaceful.

This is the act of cradling. It's how we reunite with the parts of ourselves that we like the least and with the experiences that we want the least. Cradling is one of the deepest forms of presence, as well as the epitome of self-love.

SURRENDER A STORY

Mine Your Memories (PAGE 79) *explored the creation of life stories. We tell stories not just about the past, but about the present and future as well. "I have to fight for everything I get." "Greed is destroying the world." "No one will ever really love me." A* story, *in this context, means an interpretation of a situation that we can't possibly verify. Such stories masquerade as facts. They keep us from investigating further, from accepting other possibilities, and from opening to what's beyond them. Surrendering a story is like a freeing breeze. After you do it once, it's a joy to keep going.*

The Practice:

What aspects of your life do you view through the filter of a story? Family? Relationships? World events? Choose one and articulate the story you tell about it. A story, remember, seems true but isn't verifiable. Clinging to it often keeps you shut down. Before you decide whether to let this particular story go completely, surrender it for just a day. Discover how that aspect of your life feels when unburdened by the story. If it truly does feel better, consider surrendering the story for good.

HOLLER

In De-Aggravate *(* PAGE 106 *), you soothed your aggravation at life's annoyances by connecting with the emotions that those annoyances evoked. Another way to work with aggravation is to simply holler it out. Such a release can immediately restore us to the present moment. In addition, it can feel like lifting a thousand-pound weight off our shoulders.*

The Practice:

Find a location where no one else can hear you. If one isn't readily available, use a pillow to muffle your voice. Start slowly, warming up your vocal cords with a growl. Then let that growl intensify into a full-fledged holler.

Imagine that with this holler you're voicing your displeasure at everything that has ever hurt your feelings, made you angry, or impeded your fulfillment in any way. Take frequent breaks, especially if the sound makes you a little uncomfortable or scared, but make sure you holler at high volume for at least thirty seconds. Can you feel how much pent-up energy has now begun to flow? If it feels like a lot more energy remains, consider making this a weekly practice.

CONTACT IMPROVISATION

In addition to Dance Like Mad (PAGE 19), Be Moved (PAGE 39), Spin (PAGE 66), *and* Pretend to Tango (PAGE 107), *there's another type of movement that's bound to keep you spectacularly awake. Contact improvisation is performed by two people who support and follow each other's motions while staying closely connected. They might stand, kneel, or entwine on the floor. It requires both partners to respond with care and finesse to rapidly changing bodily configurations. Once you get over beginner's jitters, contact improv can be incredibly fun.*

The Practice:

Start on the floor, in silence, right next to your partner. To get used to this unusual style of movement, roll right over each other lengthwise. Feel what it's like to support an entire rotating body. Don't let your elbows, knees, or any other sharp body parts jab your partner. Continue rolling together in different formations, letting each roll naturally lead to the next.

When the moment feels right, rise to your knees while remaining in contact. Twirl, spring, and lean together gently. Do this while you're standing as well. Then, remaining as attuned to each other's movements as possible, combine all three levels—lying on the floor, kneeling, and standing— into a dance with a life all its own.

HONOR THE TAKING OF LIFE

Every living thing must kill other living things to stay alive. That's the unavoidable cycle of nature, and it is just as true for a vegan as it is for the most inveterate meat eater. In addition to our need for food, we kill for clothing, shelter, and comfort. We also kill for aesthetics (weeds in the garden) and by accident (insects while barreling down the road). Taking life is not a problem in itself, but when we do so obliviously, it diminishes our sense of connection to life and therefore to our own aliveness. Honoring the lives we take helps to restore that aliveness and adds a sacred dimension to the ongoing pursuit of survival.

The Practice:

For one week, before you eat each meal, perform a ritual of your own design that honors what died in its preparation. You might, for example, say a word of thanks. You might set aside one forkful that is not to be consumed. Or you might simply wait silently for a whole minute before beginning to eat. Whatever ritual you create, open yourself intentionally to its effect. Let it sensitize you, for the moment and beyond, to the intricate web of existence.

When someone has wronged us or those we love, it's often extremely difficult to forgive. Yet the lack of forgiveness hurts ourselves more than anyone else because it shuts us down and renders us unable to experience all of life's ever-present joy. Willing yourself to forgive doesn't necessarily create forgiveness, however, unless you also include a willingness to feel all the emotions that might stand in your way. When this is the case, choosing to forgive is one of the greatest gifts you can give yourself.

The Practice:

Is there someone you'd like to forgive but haven't yet been able to? If so, focus on the wrong that person has done. Let all your emotions about that wrong come to the surface. Then imagine the person is right there with you. Tell that person exactly what's happening. Start each sentence with the phrase "I feel . . ." When the emotions seem too powerful to be contained by your imagination, speak the words out loud, or even yell them. You might need to perform this practice a number of times. You'll know you're all done when no strong emotions arise. In their place, forgiveness naturally occurs.

END

Everything has its season. All of creation is meant to be born, exist, and perish. Endings, seen in this way, can be as natural and beautiful as beginnings. But they're also often sad, and therefore we tend to fend them off until absolutely necessary. When doing so, we're less able to welcome all that's new, unexpected, and vital to us right now. No matter how bittersweet, every well-timed ending is ultimately a celebration.

The Practice:

Take a while to survey your life. In what part of it is something ready to come to a close? This could be a regular get-together, membership in an organization, a career path, or a personal habit. It could be something that's no longer valuable, or something incredibly valuable that has just run its natural course. Whatever you choose, let it end as peacefully as possible. To do so, incorporate all the tools of presence that you've gained from this book. Keep your mind and heart open. Be attentive to your body and ensure that it's relaxed. Be attentive to your emotions and ensure that they're flowing freely. Finally, when you know you're ready, acknowledge what's now ending with an inner bow of appreciation.

ACKNOWLEDGMENTS

This book would not have been born without the generous midwifery of Leslie Jonath. She is bighearted and wise, and she taught me an amazing way to cook asparagus.* Also essential to *How Now's* creation was my warm and skillful editor, Lisa Campbell, and my loyally enthusiastic agent, Eileen Cope.

Randi Benator helped steer me toward certain key entries. Krys Lowe suggested *Cloud Figures. Self-Acupressure* was aided by Ewald Berkers, who created and maintains a wonderful website, www.eclecticenergies.com. In addition, the actual writing of this book was graced with presence due to the enchanting encouragement of Leslie Davis.

Angels all, I honor, thank, and salute you.

Preheat oven to 500 degrees. Break off stems at bottom and lay spears side by side in glass pan. Drizzle with olive oil and sprinkle with salt. Place in oven for about ten minutes, checking along the way for desired crunch or softness. Then celebrate the moment with irresistible green delight.